T0380828

THE EVERYDAY WOMAN'S GUIDE TO ENTREPRENEURSHIP

All your questions answered, plus key brand building tools and sharable inspo pages

AuthorHouse™
1663 Liberty Drive
Bloomington, IN 47403
www.authorhouse.com
Phone: 1 (800) 839-8640

Interior Image Credit: Melissa Kingery Photography

Published by AuthorHouse 03/14/2019

ISBN: 978-1-7283-0208-9 (sc)
ISBN: 978-1-7283-0209-6 (e)

Library of Congress Control Number: 2019902279

Print information available on the last page.

This book is printed on acid-free paper.

authorHOUSE®

For my husband, Josh, and my parents, Joseph and Diane.

May every woman who turns this page come to understand her own
force to be reckoned with.

Hey there! I'm Ali, corporate-ladder-climber turned full-time freelancer. At the age of 24, I became the youngest Director of a prominent, Connecticut-based content marketing agency. Then, I launched a content marketing company from the couch of my one-bedroom apartment. Now, I serve 20+ clients worldwide based out of beautiful Southern California.

I help disruptive brands drive extraordinary outcomes as a content marketing expert, and in my spare time consult female entrepreneurs as a personal brand strategist. I love helping women discover their innermost power and confidence, which is what I firmly believe to be the most effective driver of sustainable change and long-term success.

Personal and professional growth require an environment in which we can freely experiment, loftily dream and securely course-correct. This is an inspirational guide for women with a desire to grow in life and entrepreneurship through light-hearted lessons, practical applications and tools for measurable improvement. It's for the everyday women out there (like me) who are going with the flow, surrendering to the chaos and learning along the way.

I don't make any promises with my keys to success. All I know is that the lessons I've learned have transformed my life.

Maybe they can for you, too.

XO, ali

TABLE OF CONTENTS

INTRO

I was scheduled to have coffee with an acquaintance when she messaged me the day before: "I have totally been in a funk and down on myself, so I'm not really game to talk business lately. Maybe when I decide what I want to do with myself we should get together."

In a strategy session, a brilliant female entrepreneur--a woman with a master's degree in Integrative Marketing and thousands of social followers--told me that big-name brands in her field don't pay for blogging. "It just doesn't happen," she said.

Every woman has incredible, revenue-generating potential, yet many of us measure ourselves on the wrong things. We compare. We overanalyze. It's easy for our brains to embrace a false sense of security when feeling uncertain or worried. As a result, we realize only a subset of benefits. We fail to tap into our most profound abilities. We forgo inconceivable levels of success.

I wish I could share with every woman the greatest lesson I've learned through the years: **there are no rules to life and no playbook to business.**

There's just you, and that's pretty damn powerful.

THE ONE THING THAT YOU HAVE

THAT NOBODY ELSE HAS IS YOU.

YOUR VOICE. YOUR MIND. YOUR

STORY. YOUR VISION.

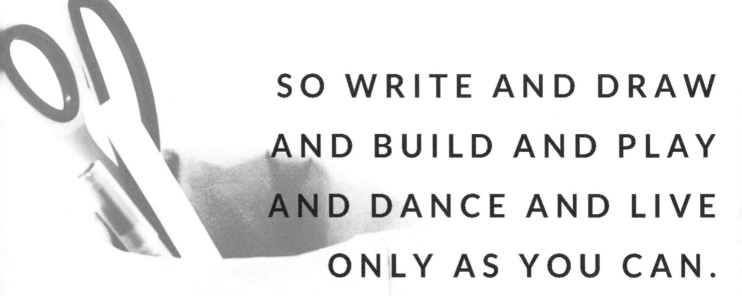

**SO WRITE AND DRAW
AND BUILD AND PLAY
AND DANCE AND LIVE
ONLY AS YOU CAN.**

THE WAY
WE GET BY

The year is 2012. I'm the youngest person working for a Connecticut-based marketing firm. After applying to more than 200 jobs, this was the only company that requested an interview. I started working as an entry-level editor five days after graduating with a bachelors in English, Writing and Mass Communications.

I didn't care if I swept the halls. I needed a job in my industry, fast. Looking back, I realize how imperative this job was for getting to where I am today. If only one other employer had agreed to an interview, my entire career (dare I say, life) trajectory would have looked different.

I took the job as a way to get by. Today, I owe it everything.

OPPORTUNITIES IN THE UNLIKELIEST OF PLACES

The story of my career beginnings is just one of endless ways life has shown me that **the greatest opportunities happen in the unlikeliest of places.**

If it wasn't for that employer, I wouldn't have been able to quickly establish my own client base as a freelancer. Allow me to explain...

As Director of a seven-person editorial team, many of my clients were understandably confused as to why I had parted ways with the company so quickly (I was laid off due to "restructuring," conveniently right before my scheduled move to California). I kept in touch with several clients and the rest is history.

I am continually astounded by life's little delights. My first client as a freelancer came not from a corporate crossover but a contact of a contact of a contact I had made years prior. I had met a woman several years earlier while out on a walk with my now husband. I asked if I could pet her dog (duh) and we struck up a conversation where I learned that she was the VP of her own marketing firm.

When I decided to go solo, I gave her a ring and she put me in touch. I have acquired new clients from thrift stores and dog parks. I have made key connections at cafes. All moments you could never plan which you'll never get back.

Because of my experiences, I firmly believe in the power of saying "yes" with an open and positive perspective.

Game-changing opportunities are the result of taking action when **others** won't bother. If you don't take initiative, someone else **will**.

SIDEBAR

Can we talk about the beauty of life's natural and inevitable design? I truly believe every moment at that marketing firm was meaningful and purposeful. Not just being hired as an entry-level editor but transitioning to the company's content marketing division. Not just being promoted to Assistant Manager but then Director of an entire team.

Every second added up to perfectly position me for the moment I never thought would come: starting my own business.

If you were to ask me then, I would have never believed in my wildest dreams that I would be doing what I am today--let alone that the opportunity would stem from where it did. Unlikely, no?

There is little I believe in as strongly as the fact that everything happens for a reason. When my mentor and former Director--a brilliant woman and inspiring leader--asked me to succeed her, my first thought was *heck* no. I didn't want the added pressures and responsibilities, and I imagined that upper management would be difficult to work with. Yet in the end, I would have regretted more not seeing what I was capable of achieving.

Even if I failed miserably, I knew I would walk away better for having seized the opportunity. Accepting the promotion ended up being one of the best and worst decisions of my life. I became depressed and wouldn't eat. I experienced physical symptoms of extreme stress. But it all lead me to where I am today, and to me that's worth it.

In looking back, I'm reminded that uncomfortable and even painful situations have their place in our purposeful path towards success. We need to trust life's plan, even if we don't understand the path.

SUCCESS ALMOST ALWAYS
HAPPENS THE WAY WE
NEVER THOUGHT IT
WOULD.

INTO THE VOID

In just one day, I had gone from Director of Content Marketing responsible for a seven-person editorial team to being by myself with my own thoughts. I went from making $75,000 a year to no sustainable income besides unemployment checks I could claim for the next six to 12 months.

I was very unhappy at my job and so I was in an odd way at peace with what had happened. I was excited about the newness of life and the possibilities that lied ahead, but I'd be lying if I said I wasn't equally scared of the void.

I had a conversation that day with a dear friend who happened to have two successful businesses of her own. In the past I had discussed with her the dream of working for myself with my own set of clients.

She told me to go for it. Then I thought to myself...

If not now, when?

So I did. I launched a website. I followed up with my clients from corporate. I designed new business cards and created fresh samples of work. I had little idea of what I was doing, but more passion and drive than ever before.

Within one week I had my first client. Within one month I had five. Now, I have over 20 clients worldwide.

You have to embrace the void in order to fill it.

I know what you're thinking.

Sure, let me just reach out to all of my clients right now. Beep boop boop ::mimicking dialing::

You might be thinking I'm out of touch or that I don't remember what it was like to start from the bottom. I haven't forgotten. I just believe in you that much. I know with absolute certainty that you can get to where you want to be because I did.

I paid $20 to launch my first website using money from unemployment checks. My brand evolved through the years to what you see today. It won't happen overnight, but I promise that with good counsel and a sincere belief in your own power and capability you can do whatever you set your mind to.

Surround yourself with the shining light of **POSITIVE THINKERS.**

People who define life and career success on their **own terms.**

'TIL YOU MAKE IT

I hate the phrase "fake it 'til you make it." What does that say about someone's passion or willingness to learn? More importantly, what does it say about their efforts? It implies you're coasting rather than climbing.

I believe that every effort and action is impactful. I believe that with hard work and dedication you can "make it," but you'll have to travel your own purposeful path for getting there. No comparisons, just you.

Define success on your own terms. Once you know what "making it" looks like for you, create a strategic roadmap for getting there. The beauty here is that there's no right answer. Maybe you won't know what "making it" looks or feels like until you reach that point. Maybe it's something you can't even comprehend yet. That's *totally okay*. You don't have to have it all figured out right now. All that matters is that you're bold enough to have a vision and brave enough to pursue it.

I know it sounds horribly cliché, but you need to trust that you'll get to where you want to be in your own perfect timing.

SIDEBAR

Why do I feel so strongly about women helping women?
Because of one woman who took a chance on me. My former
boss--the woman who I would one day succeed--saw
potential in me even at my most inexperienced.

She recognized in me strengths I never knew existed. She
saw skills that could be honed. She fought hard for my career
advancement and financial compensation. She stood up for
me when I was still learning how. She challenged and
continually encouraged me. She provided opportunities
early on in my career that most women never get.

She had a family of her own. She had her own work
responsibilities, pressures and stresses. She didn't have to
clear a path, but she did. I owe so much to her dedication to
my personal and professional growth.

Our relationship extended far beyond the office. She
attended my wedding. Today, living on separate coasts, we
stay in touch and contribute thought leadership content to
each other's businesses.

Seek out women who create space for other women. Women
who believe in the transference of power instead of wielding
theirs as a weapon to bring others down.

STAND UP

What you tell yourself is what you will achieve.

If you tell yourself no one is interested in your skills, then you won't see much demand.

If you tell yourself a certain fee is too high (within reason), it becomes so.

When I was 24 years old, I walked into my Vice President's office and told him I wanted to make $75,000 a year with my promotion to Director (a $20,000 raise). I got it, plus a new office with a window view. I became the youngest and second highest-paid Director in the company's history.

It seems crazy until you start doing it yourself. Try it out and you'll see what I mean.

The same goes for customers and prospects. **If a client is not willing to pay what you believe you are worth, have the courage to walk away.** Keep prospecting until you find customers that believe in you as much as yourself. I promise you they're out there. If your prices are not unrealistic (basic research can guide your efforts), stand up and never settle.

This also goes for work processes. Not all people will respect your boundaries. Set them anyway.

Here's a story to give you an idea of what I mean:

I had a call with a prospective client about content creation. The individual I spoke with elaborated on the company's requirements and budget. It was a perfect match on paper. Until...

"The President is a control freak. He is very impatient and needs to have things done his way. He gets easily frustrated when things don't go exactly how he wants them."

In a nutshell, I politely suggested that we may not be a good fit if this is the kind of environment they require.

It sucks to walk away from potential business, but even more to be taken advantage of.

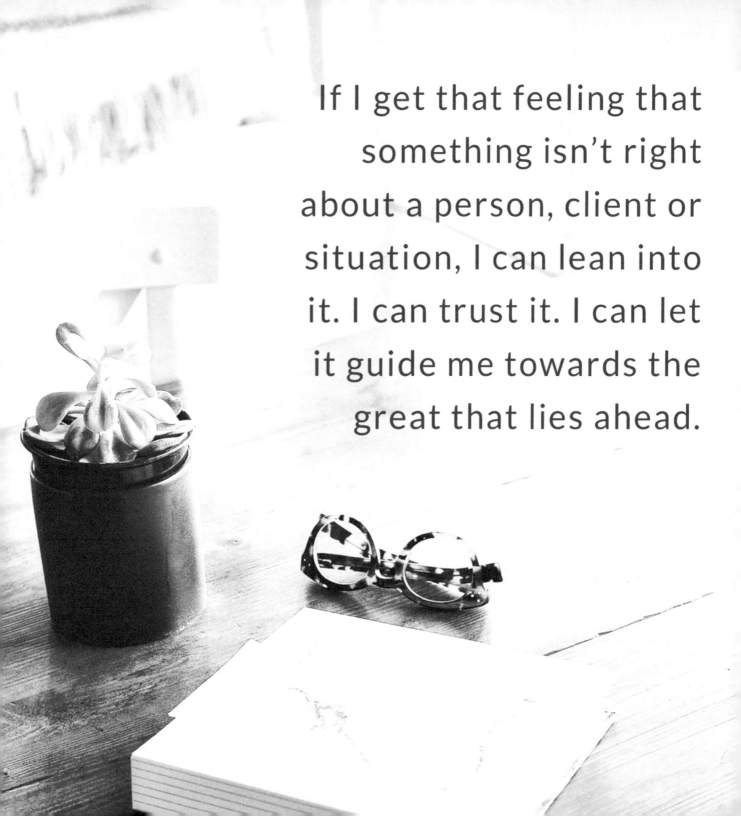

If I get that feeling that something isn't right about a person, client or situation, I can lean into it. I can trust it. I can let it guide me towards the great that lies ahead.

LEAVING CONNECTICUT

The year is now 2016. I am newly married, freshly parted with corporate, and working as a full-time freelance Content Marketer and Brand Strategist. I'm supplementing unemployment checks with income from my business. It is slowly but surely taking off.

In June, my husband and I move from Connecticut to California on a 10-day cross-country road trip. I nervously tell my clients I'm taking a two-month hiatus from work. They tell me to enjoy and they'll see me when I'm back online.

People thought we were crazy. Some family members were upset that we were "leaving them behind." But in the end I had to live life on my own terms. Eventually I came to understand that you don't need to justify yourself or your decision-making to anyone. If someone can't respect your choices, you may have to set boundaries.

In a matter of weeks I gained so much I never thought I could. I moved to a dream location, purchased my dream car (a hardtop convertible), and started a dreamy new chapter of life with my new husband.

What makes you any different from achieving those things on your dream "To Do" list? You already know the answer: nada.

What if you relentlessly pursued that idea you've been toying with for months or years, no matter how crazy? What's stopping you from doing so?

What is your "Connecticut?" In other words, what's that thing that perhaps you need to leave behind? Negative influences? Self-destructive thoughts? We owe it to ourselves to give this serious contemplation.

SIDE BAR

Remember that friend who encouraged me to go for it with my business? There were times when I was low-key jealous of her. Of course I was thrilled for her success; she was (and still is) the epitome of a badass boss.

Yet at the time of our conversation she had successfully launched multiple companies and was pregnant to boot. It was easy to feel small and defined by my inexperience. I remembered thinking, "How does she just whip up businesses like it's nobody's business?" I felt like I wasn't doing enough in comparison.

Then it dawned on me.
It *is nobody's business*, including my own!

The only difference between her and me was that she had freed herself from the restraints of conventional thinking. What *she* thinks people want her to do. What *she* thinks is expected of her.

In coming to this realization, I was able to identify and correct behavioral patterns of my own that were limiting my ability to innovate, grow and achieve.

Now people ask me how I was able to start my own podcast and launch my own line of t-shirts. It's because I had an idea and just went for it. I didn't let the fear of failing stop me from trying, and I learned much about myself and business along the way.

THE BURGER THEORY

If you have ever dieted, then you know what a cheat day is. It's a day that you allow yourself to dine on the delightfully delicious (for me, that's In-N-Out and Doritos). These are days you normally relax and don't exercise. In many ways, cheat days are self-care days (we can't always be counting calories).

Some weeks you might find you need more cheat days than normal. You might lose your motivation to eat healthy, even. The same happens in business.

It's okay if you have a "cheat day" or even a few. You might want to use downtime to relax. You may need to take a break for mental clarity. Science actually shows that the best creative insights happen during moments of disengagement and distraction. The bottom line is that you should never feel guilty for prioritizing your mental health.

Honor the necessary balance between grinding and unwinding.

When we relax, we're able to focus in a different way, attracting different energy and producing different outcomes.

REACHING
THE SUMMIT

———————

Personal and professional growth is a never-ending journey. This is a *good thing*. Be present in your current state, thankful for every moment and opportunity, and eager for all that lies ahead.

Personally speaking, I have achieved more than I could ever imagine in the last few years but have further hopes and goals. I want to become a mother. I'd like to get better at being quick to listen and slow to speak. I'd love to increase my number of speaking engagements and opportunities.

The journey doesn't end unless you say it does. Don't let it.

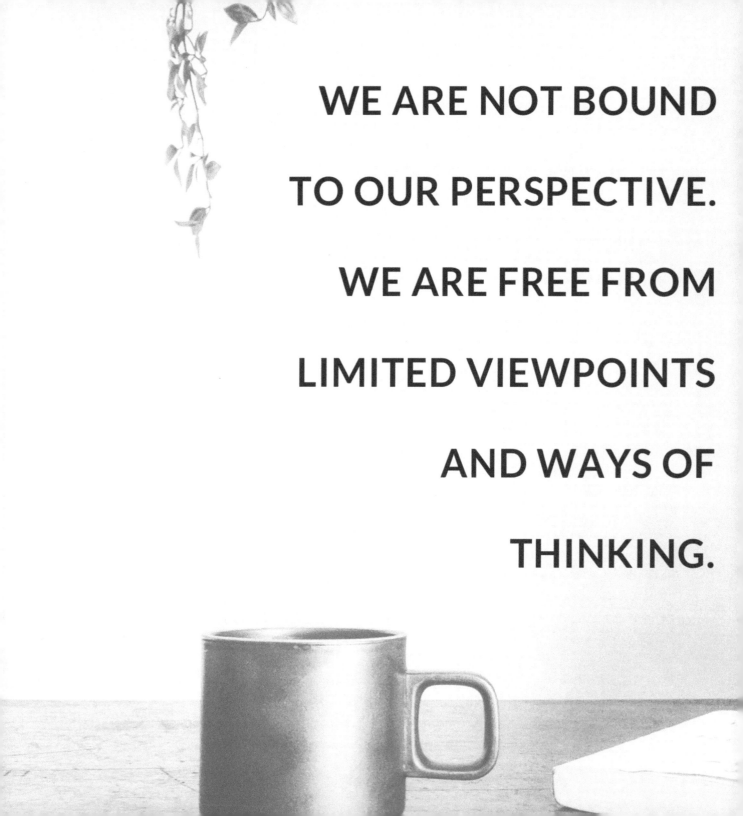

WE ARE NOT BOUND

TO OUR PERSPECTIVE.

WE ARE FREE FROM

LIMITED VIEWPOINTS

AND WAYS OF

THINKING.

Let's pause here. You know my story, now I want to know how you're feeling. Excited? Eager? Overwhelmed? Unsure?

You might be thinking, "How can I really just do this?"

This question is normal, but you can't sit on it for too long. Go back a page and re-read the quote. Now, again. This is honestly the best advice I can offer you moving forward. You must be willing to push the limits of possibility, not just in business but in your own mind.

Listen, we're not large corporations with ample spend. We're everyday women with a vision and some dollars to invest. You're going to be challenged by constraints. Instead of worrying about your limitations,
use them to your advantage. Constraints force focus and creativity. They're necessary for achieving breakthrough growth. Remember: embrace the void to fill it.

I'll leave you with this quote from Oprah: "Don't worry about being successful but work toward being significant and the success will naturally follow."

As you contemplate your journey, ask yourself what success means to you. Aim to be significant. If you deliver value to just one person, you've succeeded. And if everything comes crashing down, what's the worst that can honestly happen? The world will keep spinning and the sun will still rise. The only thing that will change is that you'll be refined into a more knowledgeable and experienced version of yourself.

Feeling better? I hope so. Now, grab a cup of coffee and see what other questions women just like you have.

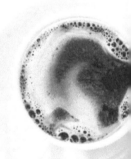

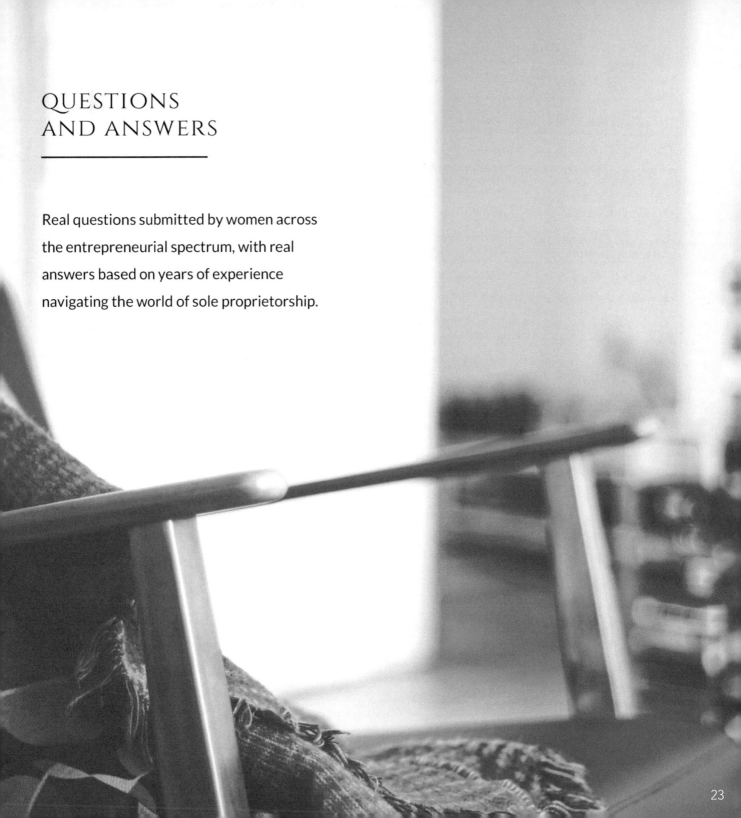

QUESTIONS
AND ANSWERS

Real questions submitted by women across
the entrepreneurial spectrum, with real
answers based on years of experience
navigating the world of sole proprietorship.

How do I decide what business to start? -*Meredith S., Las Vegas*

The best ideas come from the heart; there has to be passion behind the purpose. If you don't have a gut feeling about one particular business idea, get introspective. What are your passions? What's that one wild idea in the back of your mind? Could it be something more?

Whatever idea you land on, ensure that it is sustainable, scalable and stable. Ensure it delivers real value to a group of targeted consumers. Create a value proposition. Identify a target audience. Develop a mission and vision. Do your research, and take your time.

How do entrepreneurs start off? -*Ashley R., MN*

Trust life's natural course, follow your instincts and never underestimate the power of outreach. Every email, phone call, event and business card has a proven ripple effect. There is no bad idea when starting off as an entrepreneur; you only stand to gain.

Stay persistent, and think of ways to creatively fill the pipeline. Also reach out to every viable connection. If you lack connections, start laying the groundwork for establishing them. Go to networking events, workshops and tradeshows. Connections are *integral* to entrepreneurial success.

How can I become a successful entrepreneur with no money? -*Tracey O., CA*

It's impossible to spend nothing and become a successful entrepreneur, even if you have no employees or capital expenses. You'll likely want to be conservative when starting out (I paid $100 to launch my website and order business cards in the beginning). Spend will naturally increase as your business grows (now, I spend approximately $6,000 each year on business expenses). This includes everything from the square footage of my home office to a portion of our monthly phone and Internet bill to business cards and client lunches. Financial spend will differ depending on the market you're entering, but an upfront investment will be necessary.

How do I do something that I've never seen done before? *-Rachel C., CT*

The fact that you're asking this question means you're on the right track! Create a strategic roadmap for bringing your unique vision to life. Visualize your goals and identify incremental steps for achieving them in line with your larger, long-term plan (this includes estimated dates for task completion).

This isn't always easy (something never-before-seen requires things never-before-done). Don't rush this process. In many ways, this stage is the most important of your entire entrepreneurial journey. Don't be afraid to think big, bold, conceptual ideas.

What should I look for in people who I want to work alongside? *-Jackie C., PA*

Look for people who understand your passion and share in your vision and mission. Anyone you onboard should have an inherent understanding of your brand identity and unique value proposition. After that, find people who exhibit the qualities you admire most (i.e. good communication, organization, timeliness, creativity). Desired skills will differ depending on the market you're in.

How do I motivate myself to keep going when I'm still figuring out how to make my dream come alive? *-Heather M., CA*

Surround yourself with positive and encouraging energy. This could be your friend base, a group on social media of like-minded women, successful individuals who you admire, or the aesthetic in your home or workspace (I surround myself with positive messages to keep me in a good headspace).

Create a vision board that depicts the kind of woman or entrepreneur you want to be. Hire a photographer to take branded shots and then frame them. Create the momentum. Set the precedence. Don't be afraid to build your own beautiful, magical world. No one else will do it for you. Above all, you must constantly believe in yourself. Be your own biggest fan through the highs and lows.

How do you determine how much to charge for labor? *-Rebekah R., MA*

Research extensively. See what others in your field are charging. More importantly, understand your target audience and what they're willing to pay. I would advise starting out with more conservative rates and increasing as you gain clout.

You don't want to start too low, yet don't want to run the risk of not being paid at all. Lower prices make it easier to convert prospects into loyal paying customers. If you've charged too high, you'll quickly find out. Test the market and adapt as necessary.

Where do you start with calculating taxes? -Angela K., CA

Taxes are complicated to say the least. The amount you'll need to submit will depend on several variables. For example, if you are married and if so whether you file jointly or separately. I want to say you'll get it right the first year, but chances are you'll have to work out some kinks.

The approach that works best for my husband and I is to have our combined federal taxes deducted from his pay while I am responsible for paying our combined state taxes every year. This amount accounts for about 15% of my monthly income.

If you're not sure where to start, I would advise taking 30% off the top of every payment and adjusting the following year as necessary. This will hopefully ensure you won't owe, which is not fun (trust me). If you're operating as a sole proprietor in B2B like me, you'll need to submit W9 forms for each client and make 1040E payments. You can manually submit checks every fiscal quarter, but I've found it's much easier to pay online.

You can sign up at www.irs.gov/payments to submit federal payments anytime throughout the year. At the end of the day, the best thing you can do is find a good tax consultant!

How do you remain focused and motivated while juggling life, family and children? -Meredith S., Las Vegas

I know it sounds cliché, but when you love your business so much it doesn't feel like something you must juggle. I actually find myself having to step away from the computer in order to be present with my husband, run errands, etc. As you pursue your dream, you'll likely find that it's your personal life you must remain focused on outside of work.

At the same time, your family should be supportive of your passions and goals. That might mean your partner watching the kids while you lock yourself in your office for a few hours or traveling with you to industry events. Don't be afraid to involve family in your business when possible. Ask your hubby to give feedback on marketing materials or see what the kids think of your new product idea. This is the beauty of working for yourself: you get to have the best of both worlds!

When I was in corporate, work and personal life were treated as two separate entities. When you work for yourself (especially in a home office), you find that business and family become integrated in many ways. It's a unique transition that can be difficult at first, but after time you ease into.

For me, the greatest challenge starting out was time freedom. It was difficult for me to enjoy having so much time at my disposal versus feeling guilty for it (a product of being conditioned by a corporate environment for years). I had to rewire my brain to enjoy, and then capitalize on, the free time I was now allowed for exploring, innovating and growing.

Today, I'd say the greatest challenge is pulling myself away from the home office when I know it's always there with work to be done. When your office is so accessible and you truly love the work you do, some discipline is required to keep yourself balanced.

SIDE BAR

Let's talk some more about career and family--specifically, marriage. It takes a lot of patience and understanding to make things work, not just regarding bad habits and frustrating tendencies but hopes, dreams and goals.

My husband would disagree, but I feel most of that patience and understanding was needed on my end. Anytime I mentioned a business idea to him, he was on board with it. Podcast equipment. Fancy new business cards. The book you're reading right now.

He never discouraged me. If he had questions or concerns, he'd raise them. At the end of every discussion, he made it known that the ball was in my court. He had faith in my ability to make sound decisions that would benefit us in the long run. I recognized that privilege and never took it for granted.

Then, one day he told me he wanted to go back to school to get his degree in Electrical Engineering. I'm ashamed to admit I immediately thought of the costs. Then I realized that just as I always took careful measure before approaching him with an idea, he naturally would do the same. I raised my questions and concerns, we talked them out, and we found a way to make his dreams happen on our own terms.

You and your partner share many goals while some may be distinctly different. Stand by each other as you chase your dreams. Respect each other's perspective and trust each other's judgement.

Above all, if there's any way to make the dream happen *do it.*

How do I build clientele besides close family and friends? -Danielle G., NJ

Put yourself out there, being unafraid of the results. Reserve a booth at your town fair, for example, or exhibit at an upcoming tradeshow. If you don't have the funds to exhibit, walk the floor and network. As you prospect, work to stay at the forefront of peoples' minds through consistent, targeted engagement. Create a newsletter. Start a blog and publish content every week or month. Share relevant content across social media. Every action and interaction adds up to increase your number of qualified leads outside of family and friends.

Beware that this won't happen overnight. It has taken me months, even years, to lock in prospects. Prospecting is a long game that requires patience, persistence and faith that your efforts will eventually pay off.

What kind of title do you need for specific businesses? -Reanna P., CT

This can depend on the nature of your business, your business location and your overall goals. For example, registering as a DBA (Doing Business As) doesn't legally protect your business, but it might be required depending on where your business operates (most states require it).

If you're a sole proprietor like me, you'll need to file a DBA if you want your company to operate under a name that's not your full, legal name (i.e. Carrie's Cupcakes, Jen's Scentsations). I, for example, operate my business under my full legal name so I don't need to register as anything. Other titles like a Limited Liability Company (LLC) offer legal protection (in the case a customer sues, your personal assets are not touched). You don't necessarily have to register your business as something, so long as you comply with your city, state and industry requirements.

For more information, visit the U.S. Small Business Administration's website.

BRAND BUILDING TOOLS

———————

SAMPLE RATE SHEET

"What's your rate?" The one question that can ruin business for the unprepared. The last thing you should do is negotiate (i.e. "How does $100 for X sound?"). Instead, you should have a rate (a.k.a. price) sheet that outlines costs for specific products and services.

Consider my rate sheet. You'll see I decided to include several columns that outline such things as asset length, turnaround time and additional service details. Notice the stipulations towards the bottom for payments and expedited delivery. If you're a service provider, you'll want to clearly set expectations for clients that need services completed faster than you normally provide. Don't leave any stone unturned when it comes to explaining how and when you deliver your products and/or services.

For my rate sheet, I created the basic chart using Microsoft Word and then uploaded a screenshot to graphic design tool Canva along with my branding and logo. A rate sheet commands authority and differentiates you from competitors. It shows customers that you're serious and will not be haggled with.

Allison boccamazzo
a la carte content marketing

RATE SHEET

Product	Length	Price	Details	Turnaround time
Blog				1 week
Ghostwritten blog			Written in the voice and style of a SME/thought leader on the topic of his or her choosing. Requires a briefing.	1 week from date briefing is conducted.
*Whitepaper			Includes all necessary calls and research, as well as project outline for client approval prior to writing.	2 weeks from date outline is approved.
*Whitepaper			Includes all necessary calls and research, as well as project outline for client approval prior to writing.	3 weeks from date outline is approved.
*Whitepaper			Includes all necessary calls and research, as well as project outline for client approval prior to writing.	3-4 weeks from date outline is approved.
Web Copy				Dependent on scope of work
Social media copy			Facebook, Twitter, Instagram, LinkedIn, Google+	Dependent on scope of work
Copy editing/proofreading				Dependent on asset length
Press release				1 week, but will work to deliver more immediately if time sensitive
Email copy				1 week
Market research				Dependent on scope of work
Graphic design			eBooks, infographics, social ads, flyers, presentations, etc.	Dependent on project
Case study				1 week

If a project is needed within 1-2 business days or requiring weekend work, a 30% rush fee will be applied to total cost.
Agreeable to a net 30 or 60 by check or online platforms including PayPal (including 3% transaction fee) and Venmo.
If a project needs substantial edits, a new project fee may need to be applied.

NETWORKING
AND EVENTS

How do I find local events or places for networking with other female entrepreneurs? *-Reanna P., CT*

Strike up conversations while out and about to discover groups or events near you. This is how I caught wind of a local "Badass Business Women" Facebook group I would have otherwise never known about. Most of these groups host monthly gatherings to network in-person. If you're looking for something more involved, consider a **membership-based organization geared toward female entrepreneurs.** There are fees associated with membership for events and activities, but you'll get richer insights and more hands-on experience.

You can also connect through your **local Chamber of Commerce.** New members are usually given a platform for exposure including such things as a dedicated online listing, key networking opportunities, and a mailing list to directly market to customers who may require your products or services.

There are also national organizations with local chapters, such as the **National Association of Women Business Owners (NAWBO).** You can become a member regardless of whether you have fully established your business or not.

The truth is that the best networking opportunities are right under your nose: waiting in line at Starbucks, at the park with your kids or out on date night. When you treat every moment like a networking opportunity, the world becomes a bigger and more exciting place.

NETWORKING
AND EVENTS

Events will differ depending on the market in which your business operates. For example, if you're working to launch a clothing boutique you might want to attend Magic, the largest fashion tradeshow in the world located in Las Vegas.

Below are five events to consider attending, regardless of the size of your business or what you sell. Come prepared with branded materials including business cards, coupons and flyers. Imagine if you were to meet your highest paying customer at one of these events. What would you want their impression of you to be?

1. Annual Small Business Expo: America's #1 B2B tradeshow for entrepreneurs, hosting events in over a dozen cities nationwide. I have personally acquired clients from this event.

2. Inc. Women's Summit (NYC): The premier business conference for women entrepreneurs and business leaders for networking and brand-building.

3. Social Media Week (NYC): Insights, ideas and opportunities business leaders need to advance themselves and their organizations in a globally connected world.

4. ASD Market Week (Las Vegas): An annual event for people who are both selling and buying a wide variety of consumer goods at all price levels. Establish connections and find inspiration that can help expand your business.

5. Agenda Show (NYC and Las Vegas): Held twice a year, once on the east coast and once on the west, Agenda welcomes all business owners regardless of their position in the marketplace or reputation. Touted as a place "where passion becomes profit and the business of creativity is conducted in a truly authentic environment."

TAX WRITE-OFFS

Any qualified business expense can be written off for tax purposes, meaning it will be deducted from your gross annual income as an entrepreneur. Below is a list of expenses that can qualify as write-offs. Types of expenses differ depending on the business. Consult your tax advisor for more information.

You can create an Excel spreadsheet or running document in Microsoft Word to track write-offs throughout the year. Remember to update your list in real-time as you go along. You can manually file receipts or use electronic banking statements for reference. I personally find the latter to be more convenient.

Client lunches/dinners

Branding software/services (i.e. logo creation, social media management, professional photography)

Web hosting platforms (i.e. WordPress, Wix)

Any costs associated with computer management (i.e. Microsoft Office 365, Antivirus software, repairs, accessories)

Tax services (ex: costs associated with tax returns or amendments)

Business cards

Phone expenses, including new equipment

Work travel (gas for driving to visit clients, traveling to industry events or networking sites)

Graphic design tools

Advertising costs (i.e. Facebook Ads, commercial production costs)

Yearly Internet if you conduct any business online (portion of annual bill)

Yearly phone (portion of annual bill)

Yearly rent or mortgage (percentage of total sq. footage)

Office décor, furniture, etc.

Business holiday cards

TAX WRITE-OFFS

Reflect on business expenses you can deduct. What might they be and how much would they cost?

According to the U.S. Small Business Administration, the average microbusiness spends around $3,000 per year in operational expenses. Use this as a benchmark for measuring your own amount of spend.

_____

_____

_____

_____

_____

_____

_____

_____

LEGAL WORKSHEET

What should you be taking out for taxes? How much do you need to make as an entrepreneur to replace your day job income? What can you call your business instead of your full legal name, and how will that change how you register?

Use the following page for thoughts, ideas and questions to bring to your tax and financial advisors.

TEMPLATE MARKUP EMAIL

How and when should you do markups? *-Emma D., TX*

If you're in B2B (like me) I believe the best time to increase rates is FYQ2 (Jan-March). FYQ1 (Oct-Dec) can be stressful for companies as they review budgets and reassess what they must do to succeed in the coming year. For B2C, I don't see why any time wouldn't work as consumer finances are much more flexible.

In terms of how to do markups, be straightforward and honest about cost drivers. Below is an email I once sent to clients notifying them of an upcoming price increase as well as restructuring of my service portfolio.

Hi [client name],

I hope all is well! I wanted to bring to your attention a slight increase in pricing and restructuring of my blogging services.

Specifically, I am no longer offering separate pricing for blogs and ghostwritten blogs. Instead, all blogs will now be priced at XX per word. This reflects an increase of XX per word for standard blogs and XX per word for ghostwritten blogs. This is the only service increasing in price. Pricing for other services such as white papers, social media bundles and case studies will remain the same.

I'd like to stress that this increase is solely to maintain profit margins. Unfortunately, this is a case of having to versus wanting to. My pricing will remain fixed at this new rate for the next year at minimum.

If you foresee this to be a problem, please let me know as soon as possible before I proceed with work that's currently in the pipeline. Happy to hop on a call to discuss further if needed.

Thanks so much for your understanding and continued partnership,
Allison

TEMPLATE MARKUP EMAIL

Experiment with your own markup email (or any other important customer interaction). What should be your main talking points? How should you convey them? Get your thoughts down on paper.

_____

_____

_____

_____

_____

_____

_____

_____

_____

_____

SAMPLE EXPENSE SHEET

We're not multi-million-dollar enterprises with sophisticated expense management software (nor do we have to be). We're one-woman shows that need to manage expenses in a practical, easy-to-understand way. Enter Microsoft Excel. Yep, it can be that simple when starting out. In fact, I still use Excel to manage my expenses several years later. It's an easy way to track monthly income and calculate yearly revenue activity.

Below is a snippet of my personal expense spreadsheet. See how I have created dedicated columns for tracking projects, payments and allocations. You can also create a column for when payments are due, which I recommend when starting out. After a certain amount of time, when working with the same customers on a recurring basis, you come to memorize individual payment terms (i.e. net 30, 60).

Simple? Sure. Effective? Absolutely. There's no shame in doing things the simple, straightforward way. You can advance your approach as you grow and learn. Also, don't forget to enter full payment amounts when tracking expenses. This provides an accurate picture of gross revenue versus income after taxes.

January Client	Payment	Going towards	February Client	Payment	Going towards
Brian/Jen blogs	$1,940	RENT	VI social posts	$112	
VI social posts	$112		Karen blog	$527	
Vantage blog	$300		JT blog	$542	
VI blogs	$540		VI blogs	$540	

PERSONAL
DEVELOPMENT JOURNAL

Mental health is crucial for entrepreneurial success. It's why we seek creative outlets. It's why we strive to connect outside of work. It's why you're reading this book right now. The following pages contain exercises for stimulating and activating your personal growth and development. Create the right mindset, embrace the power of a positive perspective, and become your most confident, capable, unapologetically badass "you."

While scrolling through newsfeeds one morning I stumbled upon a remarkable story. The title of the article: *"Tenn. Woman Who Thought She Had Food Poisoning Delivers Own Baby in Turkish Hotel Using YouTube."*

In a series of tweets, Tia Freeman told her story...

How she discovered she was pregnant in her third trimester but had booked a flight to Germany to see her best friend ("ya girl was not about to waste international flight money").

How she thought she had gotten food poisoning from her on-flight salmon entrée ("where are these cramps coming from? You know what I'll just go to sleep. Sleep cures everything, right?").

How her contractions were one-minute apart by the time she got to her hotel in Istanbul for a 17-hour layover.

How she YouTubed delivery methods and cut the umbilical cord with a pair of sterilized shoe laces.

The public freaked, yet Freeman tweeted: "I still don't understand what's so shocking about my delivery story. Maybe it'll set in one day."

I love how she doesn't feel the need to explain or justify herself to anyone. She could have easily tried to make excuses for what had happened (i.e. "I shouldn't have tried to travel"), but instead owns her decision-making and embraces it for the amazing, beautiful and unconventional experience to which it led.

What's one decision you made that not many people understood or agreed with? How did you handle those reactions and/or criticism?

_____

_____

_____

_____

_____

_____

_____

We control how others make us feel. We can choose to let people hurt us or we can overlook them. How can you more boldly own your thoughts and decision-making, no matter how unusual they may seem to others?

_____

_____

_____

_____

_____

_____

_____

_____

When working for yourself, you alone are responsible for filling your cup. No one else is as passionate about your vision, nor will they fight for it as hard as you. Some people won't understand your goals; in fact, they might go out of their way to bring you down. These are people hindered by negativity. They're hurting, so they hurt. Sometimes, they can get to us. That's okay, so long as we recognize the situation and move forward.

One time when visiting Connecticut, I was told by a family member that my husband and I essentially weren't doing enough to achieve our goals.

"There's only so much we can do," I said, "we're only two people."

"That's not true," the person countered. "There's always more that can be done."

This is true, though it was not the time or place nor had I asked for this person's advice. It was an entitled statement that left me feeling depleted.

Little did this family member know that my husband and I had gone 10 months without living in the same home just so we could make more money to pay off student loan debt (we ended up paying off over $100k in two and a half years). We had put off having children to reach our financial goals. We lived with family members for nine months to save and strategize.

We had sacrificed substantially to get to where we were and had made significant gains.

I was upset and angry. With just a few words, this person made me feel like a failure. But then, I remembered that I had the power to control the narrative in my mind. I banned the negative thoughts that had started to consume me.

Little by little, the person's influence faded.

You can't control what others say and do, but you can control how you react to them. What's one situation that left you feeling upset or angry, where someone misjudged you or offered unsolicited advice?

_____

_____

_____

_____

If you could go back in time, what would you say to that person? How would you handle the situation?

_____

_____

_____

_____

List three people in your life who you believe handle and present themselves well. What do you admire most about them?

_____

_____

_____

_____

Create a mantra (a statement you can repeat to yourself) for when you encounter negativity in the future. Use this as your secret weapon.

_____

_____

_____

You can love everything about life...

Your career.
Your family.
Your friends.
Your home.
Your accomplishments and successes.

But that doesn't mean everything is always perfect.

We all have our moments.
Our challenges.
Our doubts.
Our fears.
Our insecurities.

We should, we're only human.

But don't let feelings you experience only a sliver of the time redirect your efforts. Most of them are irrational.

At best they're indicators, not predictors.

We can't deny roadblocks along the journey to success. What are three challenges you foresee over the next 12 months **in terms of personal growth and development?**

_____

_____

_____

Now, list three challenges **you foresee for your business:**

_____

_____

_____

How do you plan to overcome some of these challenges? Write down three steps you can realistically take in the next 30 to 60 days:

_____

_____

_____

It can be cathartic to write down fears, doubts and insecurities. List yours below. Use this as a safe space to channel negative energy. Write them down to make room for positive headspace, or revisit them in the future to see how you have improved. Just maybe, you'll find that there was no reason for having fears or doubts at all.

_____

_____

_____

_____

READ AND REFLECT

Read each quote, then use the blank space to reflect on what it means to you.

It's funny how we outgrow what we once thought we couldn't live without. Life keeps leading us on journeys we would never go on if it were up to us. Don't be afraid. Have faith. Find the lessons.

@high.vibrational

Be willing to outgrow yourself

@thechampagnediet

If you want to create great things, you have to maintain your vision for the future that is big and pure and beautiful

@gabriellarosie

Instead of choosing to simply exist, decide to experience life.

Decide to live.

ANONYMOUS

Act as if nothing is holding you back. The Universe rolls out the red carpet for those who commit to their dreams.

@thechampagnediet

I thought becoming myself was improving each part piece by piece. But it was finding a hidden wholeness, seeing the fractures as the design.

Brianna Wiest

49

Choose one word to define the next year of your life. Why this word? How can you keep this word at the center of your universe?

_____

_____

_____

List three goals for the next 12 months. Don't worry about how you'll achieve them. Free your mind and embrace what speaks to your heart.

_____

_____

_____

Think about where you're currently at in your life or career. How can you learn to love the place you're in and make it the best place you've ever been?

_____

_____

_____

Challenge yourself to wipe the slate clean. Think objectively about where you're at and where you want to be. What would you change? How would you do it?

_____

_____

_____

_____

ONCE YOU START LIVING YOUR BEST LIFE, YOU'LL SEE HOW MANY PEOPLE HAVE YET TO TAKE OWNERSHIP OF THEIRS.

Let's play the "what if" game, but instead of defaulting to negative scenarios consider the endless opportunities of a limitless life. One that doesn't conform to societal norms or fit in a perfectly-shaped box. Use the below space to let your wildest thoughts run free. Embrace it. Enjoy it.

COMMUNICATION CODE

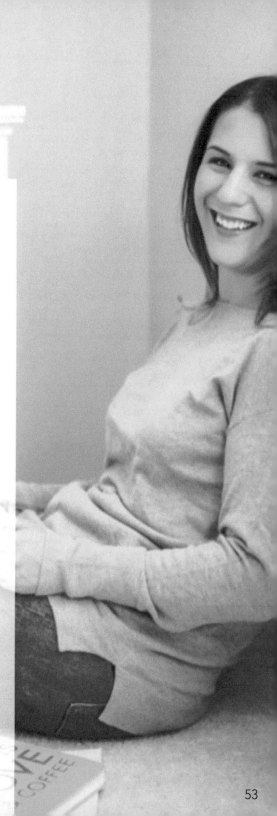

With a degree in communications, I'd be remiss to overlook the basics of customer interaction, engagement and (as much as we don't want to admit) confrontation.

When discussing business or conducting transactions, keep things conversational yet professional. Keep in mind the time of year and prioritize personal details:

"Hi [name], just checking in on that aromatherapy set you expressed interest in the other week. I'm running a great sale right now if you want to snag one. Let me know!"

"Hi [name], hope your year is off to a great start! I know you've been tied up with your kids having the bug (been there, done that!) but thought I'd just check in to see how things are going. If you still want that free sample of XX, let me know!"

Nine times out of ten, you'll get a positive response. **I cannot stress enough how crucial follow-ups are to entrepreneurial success.** Don't worry about being an annoyance. If someone is no longer interested, rest assured they'll let you know. In terms of cadence, I have found one follow-up a month to be effective.

If an issue comes up, remain professional but firm. I once had a client ask if I could work pro bono *after* I delivered a project (in other words, asking for free work after it had been completed). Here's a play-by-play of the email correspondence:

Client: "All of us are chipping in our services to gain this account. Would you please be willing to do the editing free of charge? I think we all need to have skin in the game so to speak."

My response:

"Hi [client name],

I wish we had come to that agreement prior to me spending several hours working on this. I assumed payment terms would be as usual as nothing was brought to my attention prior, and so I only think it fair that I be paid what I'm owed.

Moving forward I'm more than happy to discuss pro bono work, but it doesn't seem right in this instance having done the work expecting to be paid. I hope you can understand.

Feel free to give me a ring if you'd like to discuss further."

Client response: "I will pay the invoice, but disappointed that you are not willing to help. The check will go out in the mail this week."

My response: "I understand, and thank you for your understanding. Moving forward, I think it best that we discuss financial terms (especially something as significant as not getting paid for work) prior to beginning a project. Otherwise, I will assume all is well and that I will be compensated per my rate sheet.

As I said, I'm absolutely open to coming to an agreement that benefits us both; however, communication and transparency are key."

The client never reached back out for this project. And you know what? That's perfectly fine. The world kept spinning, the work kept flowing, and my integrity remained. Stand up for what you know you're worth. You'll never regret it.

BRANDING GUIDELINES

How do I brand myself? *-Jackie C., PA*

Branding is about creating a vibe. An experience. An escape. Your brand identity goes beyond product or service to connect with customers on a human, emotional level. This is what differentiates leaders from the masses. Your branding should be distinct while also meaningful and authentic.

Ask yourself some key questions. What colors will you primarily rely on? What will be the tone and style of your branded content (i.e. blogs, email messages, Web copy)? What kind of imagery do you want to include? More importantly, what do you want to stay away from?

Take my brand, for example. I rely on muted, earthy colors and minimalized imagery for a natural, organic feel. I try not to shy away from relatable topics that, while sometimes uncomfortable, can be useful for breaking barriers and building communities. This is my vibrational energy. It's me at my most authentic, and I've found that resonates with my audience far more than canned engagement tactics.

Outside of aesthetic, it's important that you create a mission and vision in line with your unique value proposition (why others should do business with you). My value prop is summed up as follows:

Years of corporate hustling and content management for world-leading brands have enabled me to create the perfect recipe for content marketing success: highly attentive, personalized, goal-oriented service that differentiates market positioning and customer appeal.

Your value prop is a knock-out statement that should enable anyone to quickly and easily understand your unique business model. These guidelines are imperative for creating a consistent, recognizable brand that differentiates your place in the market.

BRANDING GUIDELINES

Use this space to brainstorm branding guidelines. Think about if you were to partner with someone to expand your business. What would be general rules for them to follow to ensure a consistent, recognizable, understandable brand identity? Think about your story, mission, vision, value proposition, logo, tagline, typography, colors, imagery and more.

YEAR AT-A-GLANCE

One place for you to plan your biggest, boldest trajectory.

JAN	FEB	MARCH	APRIL
MAY	JUNE	JULY	AUGUST
SEPT	OCT	NOV	DEC

WEEKLY PLANNER

Look more closely at goals with a weekly breakdown (2 weeks' worth)

WEEKLY SCHEDULE

DATE

| MONDAY |
| TUESDAY |
| WEDNESDAY |
| THURSDAY |
| FRIDAY |
| SATURDAY & SUNDAY |

THIS WEEK I MUST

PRIORITIES

TAKE NOTE

WEEKLY SCHEDULE

DATE

| MONDAY |
| TUESDAY |
| WEDNESDAY |
| THURSDAY |
| FRIDAY |
| SATURDAY & SUNDAY |

THIS WEEK I MUST

PRIORITIES

TAKE NOTE

PROJECT PLANNER

Narrow in on specific projects. Ensure actions align with overall goals.

PROJECT SCHEDULE

PROJECT SCHEDULE

DATE	TASK	COMPLETED
		☐
		☐
		☐
		☐
		☐
		☐
		☐
		☐
		☐
		☐
		☐

DATE	TASK	COMPLETED
		☐
		☐
		☐
		☐
		☐
		☐
		☐
		☐
		☐
		☐
		☐

SOCIAL MEDIA KIT

90% of businesses use social media to increase brand awareness. Are you?

SOCIAL BEST PRACTICES

I advise clients to keep five things in mind when engaging via social media:

1. DISCLOSURE: Take careful measure to ensure opinions and statements are yours alone.

2. TRANSPARENCY: Be upfront and honest to drive loyalty and trust. If you make a mistake, admit it and course-correct immediately.

3. RELEVANCY: Always think about how you can add value by presenting meaningful and intentional ideas.

4. VALUE EXCHANGE: Embrace every opportunity to foster partnerships and exchange value.

5. PRIVACY: Do not share any information that is confidential or could compromise security.

SOCIAL CUSTOMER SERVICE

You might want to consider guidelines for delivering customer service over social media. For example:

How you wish to deal with complaints
The target response time for social customer service inquiries
A set of key messaging for dealing with the most common general inquiries
Next steps once an inquiry is addressed

CREATING SOCIAL GUIDELINES

Consider the following questions for creating your own social guidelines. Use the space below for thoughts and answers.

-What are your brand's priorities?
-What kinds of social activities would disrupt your brand's social media strategy?
-Are there any sensitive areas you need to keep in mind? (ex: points of controversy in your industry)
-What kind of image and brand voice do you want to convey?

Keep in mind your thoughts to the "branding guidelines" section on page 56!

_____

_____

_____

_____

_____

_____

_____

_____

OPTIMIZING EFFECTIVENESS

How can I most effectively use social media? *-Reanna P., CT*

Consider the following statistics for shaping an effective social strategy...

FACEBOOK:

- Most Facebook users are between the ages of 18 to 24 and 25 to 34.
- The number of Facebook users aged 65+ has increased 20% between 2017 and 2018.
- 88% of users are on a mobile device.
- Facebook users watch more than 100 million hours of video each day.
- More than 20 million businesses use Facebook Messenger to communicate with their customers.

TWITTER:

- Nearly 40% of Americans aged 18 to 29 use Twitter. That percentage drops with each subsequent age group.
- Tweets with video get six times as many retweets as tweets with photos, and are three times more likely to be retweeted than a post with a GIF.
- 74% of users get at least some of their news from the platform.
- 80% of users access the platform on a mobile device, and 93% of video views are on mobile.
- Individuals with a college degree are more likely to use Twitter.

INSTAGRAM:

- The top Instagram brands post, on average, 4.9 times per week.
- About half of businesses regularly use Instagram Stories.
- Only 20% of users are in the United States.
- The most popular Instagram hashtags are #love, #instagood, #fashion, #photooftheday, and #beautiful.
- 60% of Instagram users fall between the ages of 18 and 34.

LINKEDIN:

- LinkedIn is most popular among high-income users and college graduates.
- There are more than 20 million companies on LinkedIn, with more than 14 million open jobs.
- 79% of B2B marketers see LinkedIn as an effective source for lead generation.
- 56% of LinkedIn users visit the platform on a mobile device.
- LinkedIn SlideShare presentations reach more than 70 million unique visitors each month.

Statistics: Hootsuite

KEY INSIGHTS

What are the top things I should keep in mind when using social media? *-Jackie C., PA*

1. Know your audience to understand the platforms they're using.

2. Produce video. This can be as simple as Facebook Live or a subscription service like Promo by Slidely (highly recommend).

3. Ensure your social strategy is optimized for mobile (especially design).

4. Don't be afraid to expand your geographic reach.

5. Set up your professional Facebook page so that visitors are automatically greeted with a welcome note from Messenger. It will improve your response rate and overall brand impression.

6. Stay up to date on social trends. You can schedule posts in advance to stay ahead of weekly/monthly engagement.

NO ONE KNOWS WHAT THEY'RE DOING.

You just have to put yourself out there and give it a try.

-Reese Witherspoon

YOUR SOCIAL STRATEGY

Think about your own social strategy. What platforms are best suited for your business based on your target audience, products/services, and desired outcomes? Do you plan to engage across multiple platforms? If so, how will your strategies differ? How can you ensure you deliver the best value over social media?

Hint: think about your favorite brands and how they engage using social media. What do you like, dislike or wish there was more of? What makes you want to follow and engage with them?

SOCIAL ADVERTISING

How much should I pay for social advertising? *-Julie S., MA*

I'm going to be completely honest with you: social advertising is a large business' game. Companies like LinkedIn and Facebook tout low starting costs, but once you go down the rabbit hole you'll find advertising to be far more expensive than estimated.

Take LinkedIn. You have the opportunity to set your bid, budget and end date when using the platform's Campaign Management Tool for increased cost control. Yet the minimum daily budget is $10. That translates into a minimum of $300 per month if advertising daily, with research showing most brands set a much higher daily budget to effectively compete. Some brands allocate as much as $25 *per ad click* for optimum performance. Facebook, I have found, is no easier for entrepreneurs starting out. In fact, research shows that the average price of Facebook ads is rising around 35%, with ad impressions increasing only 10%. In other words, social advertising costs are outpacing ad performance.

I recommend three proven social advertising strategies that cost next to nothing: **influencer marketing, customer advocacy, and thought leadership.** Identify individuals who have influence over potential customers and have them organically promote your brand. Get existing customers to write rave reviews or do a testimonial blog or video. Produce content that showcases your thought leadership and expertise.

Contrary to popular belief, you don't have to spend thousands to effectively advertise your business.

BEST TIMES TO POST

What are the best times to post on social media? *-Erin H., NH*

Research suggests the best times to post across social platforms are...

FACEBOOK: Wednesday at noon and 2 p.m. and Thursday at 1 and 2 p.m. The safest times to post include weekdays from 10 a.m. to 3 p.m. Saturday has the least engagement, along with evenings and early mornings.

INSTAGRAM: Wednesday at 3 p.m., Thursday at 5 a.m., 11 a.m., and 3 to 4 p.m. and Friday at 5 a.m. are best. Thursday is the best day to post (don't forget your #TBT posts!) The safest times to post are Tuesday through Friday from 9 a.m. to 6 p.m. Sunday is the least engaging day to post.

TWITTER: The best time to post is Friday from 9 to 10 a.m. The safest times are everyday from 10 a.m. to noon. Sunday mornings receive the least amount of engagement.

LINKEDIN: The best time is Wednesday between 3 to 5 p.m. Engagement varies per day, but Tuesday through Thursday rank best. Friday through Monday receive the least amount of engagement.

Use these suggestions to identify the best times to post for your brand!

Statistics: Sprout Social

SOCIAL RESOURCES

Below are some of my favorite tools for social media and general campaign planning. Most are free and easy for beginners to learn:

Imagery: Unsplash (thousands of high-quality photos that are free to use, including for commercial purposes)

Newsletters, pop-up ads: Mailchimp (base membership is free)

Social media management: Hootsuite, HubSpot, Buffer, Google Analytics

Link shortener: Bitly

Video creation: Promo by Slidely (start for as low as $50/mo.)

Graphics creator (social posts, infographics, flyers, social media headers): Canva (base membership is free)

Website creator: WordPress, Wix, Squarespace

IN THE END

It doesn't matter how fast or slow you go, just that you keep moving. Pursue big, bold visions with practical, incremental steps. Take one day at a time, trying not to worry about all of the outcomes.

Don't be afraid to invite better things into your life. Think instead about what would happen if all your hard work paid off. Think about the kind of woman and entrepreneur you want to be today. Introduce yourself to her.

Let me be the first to welcome you to the spectacular world of entrepreneurship.

There's nothing else quite like it.

Now, for your first official assignment: share one insight you gained from this book with another woman.

Let's continue transferring power.

WISH FOR IT

HOPE FOR IT

DREAM OF IT

BUT BY ALL MEANS DO IT.

Cheers

to the person you are today.

to the person you are becoming.

to every hard-won victory.

to every purposeful setback.

to every delicious moment life has to offer.